DEDICATION

For all travelers, whether you are from outside our area or a local, I hope this gives you the inspiration to explore and try something new. Enjoy all Coastal Mississippi has to offer. We welcome you with open arms.

To Anna, for your unwavering faith that I could write this book and showcase Coastal Mississippi properly, with all its beauty and uniqueness. You are such an asset to our area, and I am eternally grateful to you. Without your constant help, support, and encouragement, this book would've been impossible to complete.

The *Nydia*

100 THINGS TO DO IN COASTAL MISSISSIPPI BEFORE YOU DIE

100
THINGS TO DO IN COASTAL MISSISSIPPI BEFORE YOU DIE

LISA EVANS

REEDY PRESS

Reedy Press
PO Box 5131
St. Louis, MO 63139, USA
www.reedypress.com

Library of Congress Control Number: 2022936993

ISBN: 9781681063829

Design by Jill Halpin

All photos are by the author unless otherwise noted.

Printed in the United States of America
22 23 24 25 26   5 4 3 2 1

CONTENTS

Music and Entertainment

Sports and Recreation

Culture and History

Shopping and Fashion

PREFACE

First, let me say thank you for taking the time to read about one of my favorite places in the world—Coastal Mississippi.

Originally from Central New York, when I relocated to Coastal Mississippi, I became known as a "Damn Yankee." That means I came to the area from the North and stayed. I stayed because I fell in love with Coastal Mississippi. Its temperate weather was a huge selling point for me at first, but then I began to discover so much more.

There is natural beauty in abundance. There is the history of the area surrounding you at every turn. Some restaurants have been on the Coast for generations. There is culture and local lore. There is a myriad of fun, family-friendly activities to suit any interest. There is proximity to the Mississippi Sound and the Gulf of Mexico and some of the most breathtaking sunrises and sunsets you will ever see. There is Southern hospitality.

Coastal Mississippi has become home for me. As I was not born and bred here, I have the advantage of not taking the area for granted. I am not jaded to its charms. I hope this book will entice you to visit us if you live elsewhere in the world. If you are local, my hope is you will find something within the book that will help you rediscover the gems at your fingertips.

Whatever your situation, may you find the desire to explore and enjoy Coastal Mississippi.

Many thanks to all who helped me gain the experiences necessary to compile this book and my family, who offered encouragement and critique in equal measure. A special thanks to Coastal Mississippi (our tourism board). With all your hard work and love for the area, you do the Coast proud!

One Thirty-One Lameuse

FOOD AND DRINK

GOBBLE UP FABULOUS CRUST AND TOPPINGS

AT POP'S PIZZERIA

Pizza is the one dish that seems universally recognizable. It has become a favorite of many. At Pop's Pizzeria, you will taste why. Here you'll find delicious food served in a casual, friendly restaurant. Locally owned and operated, this family-run business is all about pizza excellence with a welcoming vibe. As you walk in the door, the aromas coming from the kitchen will charm you. It's a bustling place on most days, but there is restaurant and bar seating. Whether you're meeting friends after work or bringing the family to a pre/post-game celebration, you will feel at home. Your meal will be remarkable, no matter what you order. Try the Margherita or the Carnivore pizza but know there are so many others to choose from. Also gracing the menu are fried pickles, homemade meatballs, an Italian sub, garlic knots, and a chicken Alfredo bake. The list is long, and nothing disappoints.

921 Cedar Lake Rd., Biloxi, 228-227-6473
popspizzeria.com

Pizza from Pop's Pizzeria

2

INDULGE YOURSELF IN CASUAL ELEGANCE

AT ONE THIRTY-ONE LAMEUSE

When you want a small, elegant restaurant with casual comfort, you'll love the way One Thirty-One Lameuse envelops you upon arrival. The food is simply excellent! Because every menu item uses fresh local seasonal ingredients, their offerings sometimes change based on availability. This cuisine is unique, innovative, and designed to perfection. Delight in sweet potato beignets, duck poppers, plum and halloumi salad, and sticky Barq's pork banh mi, just to name a few menu favorites! The chef is always creating something new and exciting. Desserts are as tasty as the main event. You will want to try the strawberry shortcake when it's in season. It's a tower of lusciousness! Or perhaps the key lime pie. The restaurant is available for private functions, and they also host many events, such as jazz brunch, "Wine Down Wednesdays," and gospel brunch.

131 Lameuse St., Biloxi, 228-207-1689
facebook.com/onethirtyonelameuse

TIP

Remember, ingredients are sourced fresh and are dependent on the season, but everything is simply fabulous. If you decide on Jazz Brunch, be sure to try the Bloody Mary. It is truly delicious!

3

SATISFY YOUR OYSTER CRAVING
AT HALF SHELL OYSTER HOUSE

Are you an oyster lover? Half Shell Oyster House is the place to be! Bringing some New Orleans flair to the Coast, people flock here to try the various dishes offered with class and consistency. Fresh oysters are served either raw or char-broiled over an open flame with your choice of toppings. Sitting and watching the shuckers work while engaging in conversation is fascinating and gives one a tremendous appreciation of their trade. Patrons can be comfortable and casual at the bar or have a business dinner or date night in the dining area. While oysters are an anchor, there is also a very diverse menu of other succulent dishes. Try a hand-cut steak, crab claws, Royal Red shrimp, seafood gumbo, or perhaps one of their specials. The high-end bar of beer, wine, and spirits will complement your meal and top off your visit!

125 Lameuse St., Biloxi, 228-432-5050
2500 13th St., Gulfport, 228-867-7001
halfshelloysterhouse.com

TIP

Being a very popular restaurant on the coast, Half Shell is usually quite busy, sometimes with lines out the door. If you want a quieter time (relatively speaking), try mid Saturday afternoon. Same great food and atmosphere, slightly less busy.

4

SAMPLE SOUTHERN FLAIR
AT MURKY WATERS BLUES AND BBQ

Are you craving some good ol' Southern barbecue? Murky Waters Blues & BBQ has got you covered. Its Gulfport location is in a historic building downtown, just steps away from Fishbone Alley. With an indoor stage, dining, and outdoor space, it's the perfect venue for a relaxing evening with family and friends. The Ocean Springs location is amid the hustle and bustle along Government Street. The charming indoor dining and a large patio and outdoor stage offer a unique ambiance. Kick back and enjoy all your favorites in barbecue—pork, brisket, and chicken—as well as juicy burgers, tender steaks, and a cold brew to top it all off. The variety of beer on tap sometimes changes as they offer well-known brands and several IPAs and favorites from local breweries. It's a hometown hangout with a great deal of personality.

1320 27th Ave., Gulfport, 228-214-4420
1212 Government St., Ocean Springs, 228-215-1114
murkywatersbbq.com

5

DEVOUR IN DELIGHT
AT TATO-NUT DONUT SHOP

Some folks might claim that donuts are all the same or that the best ones are from those fancy national chain coffee shops. Then you try a donut from Tato-Nut Donut Shop, and the taste will forever alter your palate. Your expectation of what a good donut is will change. Sounds dramatic, right? But I assure you it's true. The donuts you will find at Tato-Nut are, in a word, divine. The recipe for these various flavors of cake donuts is truly a secret. This family-run business has been on the Coast for decades, and only select family members know how to make the donuts. Everything made here is fresh daily, and, on some days, these donuts don't last long. So get there early and buy multiples of your favorite ones. Perhaps these will be glazed, chocolate, or blueberry. Who knows? Coffee and other drinks are available too.

1114 Government St., Ocean Springs, 228-872-2076
facebook.com/thetatonutdonutshop

6

SAVOR SUCCULENT SEAFOOD
AT THORNY OYSTER

You will find Thorny Oyster situated inside the beautifully designed Pearl Hotel. This high-end restaurant in Bay St. Louis's thriving downtown skillfully combines local ingredients and innovative ideas to craft a sophisticated menu. The restaurant is steps away from the water and has gorgeous views. Patrons enjoy the elegance of the raw bar, which serves up dishes such as Gulf shrimp, grouper, and ceviche. Enjoy an entrée of red snapper almondine or flounder caddy. Then top it off with a piece of Peanut Butter Icebox Pie.

Share some mussels and fries with other members of your party.

Thorny Oyster provides a venue for a special-occasion meal or perhaps a celebration among friends. Whatever the focus, you won't be disappointed. The menu is adventurous, with choices you may not find elsewhere, all served in comfortable yet elegant surroundings.

104 N Beach Blvd., Bay St. Louis, 228-688-0401
thornyoysterbsl.com

OTHER NOTABLE SEAFOOD RESTAURANTS

McElroy's Harbor House
695 Beach Blvd., Biloxi, 228-435-5001
facebook.com/mcelroys.harborhouse

Felix's Restaurant & Oyster Bar
942 Beach Dr., Gulfport, 228-284-3710
felixs.com

Cuz's Old Time Oyster Bar & Grill
108 S Beach Blvd., Bay St. Louis, 228-467-3707
cuzsbsl.com

7

CHILL OUT WITH FRIENDS

AT OLE BILOXI FILLIN' STATION

When visiting a new area, you always hear the same advice: go where the locals go. Ole Biloxi Fillin' Station is the quintessential town hangout. Set in a remodeled gas station, here you will see the overhead doors from the former garage, along with other memorabilia.

Even with a small bar, limited indoor seating, and a modest-size kitchen, the folks at the Fillin' Station churn out some great food. There is an outdoor patio area for more seating, which many patrons find advantageous. On weekends during crawfish season, you will find this area jammed with those wanting a taste of some fresh mudbugs.

The atmosphere may be casual, but don't discount the phenomenal food. Here you will find one of the best roast-beef po'boys on the Coast. Be sure to have a pile of napkins nearby—you'll need them! Another great dish: either chicken or crawfish nachos. Fabulous!

692 Howard Ave., Biloxi, 228-435-2522
facebook.com/olebiloxifillinstation

PICK UP SOME ISLAND VIBES

AT THE BLIND TIGER

What happens when someone studies under Emeril but loves the Caribbean islands and Bahamas? A restaurant named The Blind Tiger is born! Their locations offer simply amazing views in an open-air eatery, with fresh, fabulous food. In short, they are laid back with terrific food.

The staples to be found here are beer, burgers, tacos, and shrimp. Everything served is fresh—truly. These establishments don't have freezers! All the food is new each day, whether it's burgers or seafood. Patrons can order standard items each visit, but the menu specials change daily based on availability. There are no printed menus. As you walk in, check out the chalkboards.

Inside dining is offered, with windows open toward the water, allowing the ocean breezes to wash over you. Weather permitting, I suggest you head outside to soak up the sun.

119 N Beach Blvd., Bay St. Louis, 228-216-2600
265 Beach Blvd., Biloxi, 228-207-5240
theblindtiger.biz

9

SIP A PERFECT CUP OF JOE
AT THE MOCKINGBIRD CAFÉ

In 2005, nature took much from Coastal Mississippi. But good overcomes adversity and breeds love, loyalty, and community. The Mockingbird Café is the epitome of all the above. After the turmoil left behind by a lady named Katrina, the Bird (as it's lovingly called) arose from the ashes. Locals and volunteers found comfort and some peace in gathering here.

Still a beloved gathering spot, the Mockingbird Café serves some of the absolute best coffee and tea on the Coast. It offers breakfast, lunch, or brunch until 2:00 p.m. daily. Everything served is homemade, with friendliness such as a caring smile to further brighten your day. Try a Belgian waffle or a fried chicken biscuit. Or perhaps a Summer Garden Burger or Frittata of the Bay.

The Mockingbird Café takes a stand against plastic pollution. All to-go orders leave in a biodegradable cup, container, or bag. They are plastic-free.

110 S 2nd St., Bay St. Louis, 228-467-8383
mockingbirdcafe.com

10

ENJOY SUPERB FOOD
AT SHAGGY'S

Another dream realized after great hardship is that of Shaggy's. Owned and operated by a couple of Coast residents, Shaggy's now has multiple locations in Coastal Mississippi where you can enjoy great food and drinks in a comfortable beach setting.

This friendly venue proves that casual dining can be impressive! With a menu consisting of stuffed avocado, seafood mac and cheese, mahi-mahi tacos, Royal Reds (shrimp), or a good old-fashioned Shaggy's Famous Cheeseburger, you can't go wrong. A bonus to go with your meal is a spectacular view!

Whether it's a midday lunch between excursions, dinner before a walk on the beach or a night at the casinos, or a private event, you will find Shaggy's to be the perfect backdrop. With indoor and outdoor seating available, you will have an enjoyable experience no matter the weather.

120 Hiern Ave., Pass Christian, 228-452-9939
1724 E Beach Blvd., Gulfport, 228-241-1007
1763 Beach Blvd., Biloxi, 228-432-5005
shaggys.com

11

TRY SOMETHING NEW AND REFRESHING
AT VESTIGE

Have you experienced a restaurant with a preset tasting menu? How about a restaurant honored with an award from the James Beard Foundation as a finalist for the "Best Chef" category? We have such a treasure here on the Coast, a place named Vestige.

Vestige serves contemporary American cuisine in a charming setting. As a business that believes in utilizing locally grown, seasonal foods, it frequently changes its menu items based on availability. The owner-chef takes pride in developing exclusive dishes that reflect the flavors and techniques of Japan, where his lovely wife grew up. She makes all the bread and desserts, using nature as her inspiration.

Sample menu items may include a smoked oyster Bavarian tartlet, pan-seared salmon, Wagyu beef, or pumpkin challah. Visit Vestige for one of the best unique dining experiences available. Without a doubt, you will rave about it to all who will listen.

715 Washington St., Ocean Springs, 228-818-9699
vestigerestaurant.com

12

GET TROPICAL INSPIRATION
AT HUCK'S COVE

At the mouth of Mary Walker Bayou and the West Pascagoula River, you will find Coastal Mississippi's answer to those longing for a tropical vibe. Huck's Cove is a hip, neighborly stop where visitors can absorb a Caribbean-tinged feeling.

At this waterfront marina bar and grill, you can gorge on some fabulous burgers, along with some wings or tater skins. Perhaps you'd like some soft-shell crabs or a shrimp po'boy. The menu is varied, leaning toward casual cuisine. There is a wide variety of local and domestic beers and wines to enjoy.

You will likely enjoy some live music or other events during the season. But you'll always have some excellent island music to entertain you while you are relaxing and enjoying a meal and libations with family and friends. As a bonus, Huck's is now an official dog-friendly restaurant, so bring Fido along!

3000 Oak St., Gautier, 228-497-4309
huckscove.com

13

DAZZLE YOUR TASTE BUDS
AT MARY MAHONEY'S

Have you ever been dining in a restaurant only to look up and see a celebrity, such as a sports figure or even a president, casually stroll past you? At Mary Mahoney's, this has happened on numerous occasions. Family-owned and -operated since 1964, Mary Mahoney's has such a stellar reputation that it is renowned across the entire country.

Located in an elegant building, circa 1737, Mary Mahoney's offers a fine-dining restaurant with a hometown feel. Patrons run from visitors to hard-working local families, treating themselves to lunch or a special-occasion meal, to famous faces including actors, musicians, and writers.

Try some of the famous Seafood Gumbo or a signature creation like the Sisters of the Sea Au Gratin. Perhaps a perfectly cooked prime rib or whole broiled flounder. It's that good! Whatever dish you choose will leave you planning your next trip back.

Highway 90 and Rue Magnolia, Biloxi, 228-374-0163
marymahoneys.com

REVIVE YOURSELF WITH FOOD AND DRINK AT PATIO 44

Are you looking to enjoy some local favorites in an easygoing atmosphere? A perfect place would be Patio 44. Born from a chance meeting of old friends, Patio 44 serves a chef-inspired menu sourced from ingredients within Mississippi's Gulf Coast and Delta regions.

Sitting outside on the patio offers patrons a delightful outdoor dining experience while still sheltered from the weather. The gorgeous fountain offers trickling water as relaxing scenery for your meal. Revel in dinner dishes such as blue crab fondue, blackened shrimp tacos, or a juicy ribeye. Are you arriving during lunch? No problem! Try the pimento cheese sandwich or pasta jambalaya.

Another reason to visit Patio 44 is to sample its exceptional array of spirits, wine, and beer. Try a glass of Tintero Moscato d'Asti or one of their cocktails such as a mixed berry mojito, Moscow mule, or a simple Abita Amber beer. Relish the moment!

124 Main St., Biloxi, 228-207-2628
1244 24th Ave., Gulfport, 228-265-7101
patiofortyfour.com

SCARF UP GOOD OL' GRILL FAVORITES
AT FAT BOTTOM BARBEQUE

Southern barbecue is a staple in Coastal Mississippi. In this competitive category, there is no mistaking the mouth-watering dishes served at Fat Bottom Barbeque. This place does BBQ right every time. Even before you take your first bite, the aroma permeating the air wafting from the kitchen will have you salivating!

Fat Bottom Barbeque smokes all its meats over pecan wood and slathers them with a dry rub spice whose ingredients are a well-kept secret.

Situated directly on the beach, this restaurant offers diners the enjoyment of great food and a spectacular view of the water and all its nuances. All your favorite BBQ dishes are available: ribs, brisket, wings, pulled pork, or chicken. Fat Bottom Barbeque also offers many side dishes, including baked beans and potato salad. The samplers are the best: a little bit of everything!

1785 Beach Blvd., Biloxi, 228-456-0055
fatbottombarbeque.com

16

TASTE SOME HISTORY WITH A GREAT MEAL
AT SCRANTON'S RESTAURANT

Would you enjoy the experience of dining in a historic building from the early 1920s that was once the town's firehouse and city hall? If that sounds interesting, head over to Scranton's Restaurant.

Of course, it takes more than a charming location to win a robust local following. Scranton's does it again and again with its superlative take on down-home Coastal Mississippi cooking. Scranton's serves delicious meals with their local panache. Try such dishes as their shrimp gumbo, She-Crab soup, or the fresh catch of the day. Maybe grab a burger, po'boy sandwich, or some shrimp and grits. Have your favorite drink at Scranton's famous Happy Hour.

A great new concept Scranton's has developed is its take-home Market Meals, an array of casseroles and other dishes that you order and take home for dinner. They come with easy reheating directions to make dinner at home a treat.

623 Delmas Ave., Pascagoula, 228-762-1900
scrantons.com

17

INDULGE YOUR SENSES
AT WHITE PILLARS

Southern hospitality is taken very seriously at White Pillars. This restaurant has acquired many "Best Of" accolades in various categories. You will find this reflected not only in the preparation of its menu items but also its décor and ambiance.

White Pillars' owner meticulously plans your dining experience down to the surrounding artwork, all from Mississippians. This includes paintings and metal sculptures. You'll appreciate the difference, from the dishes and serving pieces to the gorgeous, handcrafted oak tables. As for the food, all ingredients are locally sourced to bring the farm-to-table experience to all guests.

The chef, who also happens to be the owner, was recently recognized as a James Beard Foundation semifinalist for "Best Chef." He serves up succulent dishes such as duck breast and crispy confit as well as various grilled fish, chicken, and steaks. This is an experience you won't want to miss.

1696 Beach Blvd., Biloxi, 228-207-0885
biloxiwhitepillars.com

FEAST
AT JOURDAN RIVER STEAMER

Are you in the mood for some of the finest in fresh seafood and steaks on the Coast? Head up to Jourdan River Steamer. You can even arrive on your boat. Pull right into the dock, no problem.

In 2018, one too many storms provided the incentive to rebuild and update. Today, the lovely building gives you windows galore to take in the beauty of the surroundings.

Jourdan River Steamer has clientele who arrive in shorts and flip-flops, as well as gowns and tuxedos. All are welcome to partake in a delicious meal that will delight your senses. Here, only the freshest seafood is served, including live Maine lobster, jumbo king crab, Royal Reds, and Dungeness snow crab. Or cut into a certified Angus Beef steak cooked to juicy perfection. You can also get pasta dishes, combination platters, and they even have a kid's menu. Prepare for the extraordinary.

15152 Mississippi 603, Kiln, 228-255-7333
jrsteamer.com

GRAB A LOCAL BEER
AT LAZY MAGNOLIA BREWERY

Craft breweries have become very popular in the past several years. On the Coast, you can explore Lazy Magnolia Brewery, Mississippi's oldest packaging brewery. Opening in 2005, it was the first brewery here since the Prohibition days of yore.

Indulge yourself in the taproom, known as The Porch. Here is the place to enjoy some craft beer with family and friends in a great setting. Charm and hospitality are the name of the game. Lazy Magnolia does offer tours and has weekly events at The Porch. Try one of the varieties of brick-oven pizza offered. They're delicious!

Lazy Magnolia has three series of craft beers. The Porch series are lower in alcohol and easy to drink. The Back Porch series are fuller-bodied brews that are higher in alcohol. The Debutante series are unique brews that take a while to mature.

7030 Roscoe Turner Rd., Kiln, 228-467-2727
lazymagnolia.com

20

MANGIA! EAT HEARTY
AT SALUTE ITALIAN SEAFOOD RESTAURANT

Casual fine dining is prevalent in Coastal Mississippi, and Salute Italian Seafood Restaurant is another place to add to your repertoire. Sit among lofty oak trees on the patio with a water view. Or if you'd like, indoor seating is spacious and comfortable.

The cleverly designed open-style kitchen entices your senses with the fragrance of fresh herbs and spices when you walk into the restaurant.

Salute offers delectable Italian dishes and local favorite seafood fare in its extensive menu. Also available is an impressive wine list that will perfectly complement any meal.

Traditional Italian dishes such as lasagna, manicotti, and eggplant parmigiana are available. Looking for something else? No worries. Try the veal or chicken marsala, or perhaps the crabmeat fettucine or shrimp scampi basilico. Whatever you choose, you will be delighted and want to visit again for more.

1712 15th St., Gulfport, 228-864-2500
saluteitalian.com

Fishbone Alley Downtown Gulfport
Photo courtesy of Alex North

MUSIC
AND ENTERTAINMENT

CELEBRATE COOL MUSIC
AT GROUND ZERO BLUES CLUB BILOXI

One of Coastal Mississippi's newest live music venues is the highly anticipated Ground Zero Blues Club Biloxi. Open since February 2022, Ground Zero brings blues musicians in from all over the country. The Biloxi club is the second highly regarded club co-owned by famed actor Morgan Freeman, a Mississippi native.

Ground Zero is a beautiful addition to the Coast's entertainment offerings. Old concert posters, ticket stubs, and other memorabilia from legendary performances at the original club adorn the building. Inside, a replica porch also mimics the original Clarksdale, Mississippi, location. This décor reminds visitors of the rich blues history throughout the state.

This club offers varied food and beverages. Try a signature cocktail (like the Juke Punch Jam), local craft brews, or other beer and wine offerings. Check it out—you'll love it! Tickets for upcoming events are available on the club's website.

814 Howard Ave., Biloxi, 228-910-6600
groundzerobiloxi.com

TIP

If you need a unique, tasty snack to accompany your meal or to munch on before a show, try The "Morgan" Special. This delightful dish is a combination of flavors: mashed potato barrels, bacon, cheddar, GZ pulled pork, sour cream, chives, and Jim Beam's Devil's Cut BBQ sauce. Believe me, you won't be disappointed!

EXPLORE YOUR FUNK
AT FISHBONE ALLEY

Started as a community project, Fishbone Alley brings a fashionable vibe to what once was an alley between two buildings used for trash and maintenance.

Located in the heart of downtown Gulfport, Fishbone Alley is now a fabulous attraction showcasing some hip art and incredible live music. You will find exciting expressions of paintings, graffiti, and murals on the alley walls. It is an artistic delight. Several live music events take place here throughout the year. Weekends usually house the most activity here, but even if you're strolling through on a quiet day, take the time to appreciate the imaginations of others.

While enjoying the area's ambiance, know there are plenty of places where you can secure some food and libations. The alley backs up into several bars and restaurants downtown. You will have your choice, only dependent on your mood.

1301 26th Ave., Gulfport
facebook.com/fishbonealleygulfport

23

DROP BY
ARTSY DOWNTOWN OCEAN SPRINGS

Downtown Ocean Springs has an eclectic mix of businesses. These include many shops, eateries, bars, art museums, and very distinct places to stay. With all the activity, one would expect robust entertainment to be a part of the culture. You would be correct.

Start your day visiting the farmers market on the weekend. Then stroll through the streets of Ocean Springs, experiencing the variety of places to explore no matter your mood. You may find yourself wandering wistfully in a toy store, then grabbing lunch a few doors down. From there, enjoy a local live band and buy some pottery for a friend. Enlighten yourself with a trip through a museum. Finish off your day with some steak, wine, and more live music.

Spend a few hours or a day—anything is possible!

downtownoceansprings.com

GET CHARMED
BY DOWNTOWN BAY ST. LOUIS

Bay St. Louis is the ultimate delightful experience. Voted the 5th Best Small Coastal Town by *USA Today*, this place has a downtown where you will find much to enjoy.

Start with the walking and biking tour, learning snippets about much of the city's history. Depending on the time of year, you may experience the 2nd Street Art Walk, where there are several family-friendly happenings, music, and other special events. Perhaps you'll stay at a fabulously beautiful, award-winning bed-and-breakfast steps away from the water. Live music, parades, and shows from the Bay St. Louis Little Theater are viable options. Don't forget to take some time to stroll along the waterfront while enjoying the views of the Bay of St. Louis and catching a stunning sunset.

A booming downtown helps make Bay St. Louis a remarkable place to spend some time.

baystlouisoldtown.com

ENJOY FOOD, MUSIC, AND WHISKEY
AT JACKS BY THE TRACKS

Looking for a change of pace? Head into Pascagoula to Jacks by the Tracks. Located in a building with many stories to tell, Jacks serves "Southern"-style sushi, tacos, salads, po'boys, and other dishes, all in the light of a tiny red stage. This stage has hosted a slew of some of the most notable musicians along the Coast.

Music lovers from all around venture to Jacks by the Tracks for fun and festivities. Catch some classic rock and blues featuring local singers and songwriters. Many popular bands play to a mixture of regulars and visitors, from people new to the area to lifelong residents. So have some fun and enjoy some good times. Try some sushi with your beer and whiskey. Bring some friends to have a good relaxing time. What more could you ask for?

709 Krebs Ave., Pascagoula, 228-334-2337
facebook.com/jacksbythetracks

26

START YOUR WEEKEND RIGHT
AT BILOXI FIRST FRIDAYS

On the first Friday of most months (weather permitting), Biloxi's downtown hosts merrymaking for all ages. Among the blend of historic and renovated sections of Rue Magnolia and Water Streets, you may well see a parade or a block party. There will be food and beverages, live music, and arts and crafts vendors. Old and new friends get together to relax after a long week.

Much planning goes into this event each month. The music offered changes each first Friday, ensuring locals and visitors enjoy a unique experience. Surrounded by a host of bars and restaurants, you can easily extend the evening with a night on the town.

Should you be in town during some special dates on the calendar, the excitement gets even livelier. Think Mardi Gras season, St. Patrick's Day, or the Fourth of July!

mainstreetbiloxi.com

COASTAL MISSISSIPPI IS KNOWN FOR ITS MANY FESTIVALS. BELOW ARE JUST A FEW. CHECK THEM OUT!

Cruisin' the Coast takes place every October. It is coastwide fun of sock hops, block parties, and cool classic cars. Cruise Central is at Centennial Plaza #66 and the Swap Meet is at Mississippi Coast Coliseum #28

The Peter Anderson Arts Festival takes place in November and celebrates art in many forms throughout the streets of Downtown Ocean Springs #23

During the **Fall Muster**, held each October, you can relive a Civil War Battle at Beauvoir #68

Enjoy the **Christmas Season** with beautiful displays throughout all the coastal cities and downtown areas, as well as the huge display called Gulfport Harbor Lights.

Coastwide **Mardi Gras Celebrations** take place during the season with parades, parties, beads, and King Cake.

During the **Crawfish Music Festival** every April, you can suck on some crawfish and dance to some music at the Mississippi Coast Coliseum #28

The **Blessing of the Fleet** takes place each spring, prior to the opening of shrimp season, for a weekend of fun celebrating the hard-working seafaring men and women and offering them blessings for a prosperous season. It is organized by the Maritime & Seafood Industry Museum #69

The **Hummingbird and Nature Festival** takes place generally each September as the tiny creatures are migrating through the area. A great way to spend time in nature at the Pascagoula River Audubon Center #46

The **Seafood Festival** is held each September on the Biloxi Town Green. It is a celebration of the rich seafood heritage in Coastal Mississippi. There are arts and crafts, dozens of food vendors, and live entertainment.

27

TAKE IN THE VIEWS AND BREWS AT SKY BAR BILOXI

What could be better than some music and fun with friends? Enjoying the same with our stunning Coast as your view, that's what! Sky Bar Biloxi is located three stories up, with an open-air concept overlooking the beach. The variety of 30 beers on tap, including some very popular local brews, ensures you won't go thirsty. Nor will you go hungry here thanks to some specialty dishes and local seafood. Complement all that with a band stage and DJ booth, and you've got yourself a party. You'll find a pool table, a dartboard, and friendly, engaging staff members.

The *pièce de résistance* is the gorgeous view of the water and all its nuances, from bright sun to twinkling stars. You'll find enjoyment and that view whenever you visit! Watch the beachgoers or watch the sunset. Finish it off with live music on weekends and when special events are happening on the Coast.

1749 Beach Blvd., Biloxi, 228-206-7075
skybarbiloxi.com

28

THRILL TO A CONCERT
AT THE MISSISSIPPI COAST COLISEUM

As one of the premier venues in our area, the Mississippi Coast Coliseum & Convention Center is host to diverse concerts and other special events that draw thousands of patrons to the Coast looking for entertainment.

Overlooking the beach, with both indoor and outdoor venue space, the Coliseum offers not only top-notch events but a dazzling view of the coastal waters while you attend them. Concerts such as Reba McEntire, Cher, KISS, Elton John, Luke Bryan, Chris Stapleton, Jamey Johnson, Lil Baby, Kevin Gates, and many others show the broad expanse of musical acts hosted here. Other events like the PCA Rodeo, Disney on Ice, and Monster Jam add to the list.

Being actively involved in community events, such as high school and college graduations, makes the Coliseum an intrinsic part of Coastal Mississippi. Take a moment to see what's happening here while you're in town.

2350 Beach Blvd., Biloxi, 228-594-3700
mscoastcoliseum.com

LEARN ABOUT A MUSIC GENRE
ON THE MISSISSIPPI BLUES TRAIL

Tightly woven together are Mississippi and blues music. The blues is the foundation of numerous music genres. Traveling to spots along the Mississippi Blues Trail will give you an overwhelming desire to learn more about it.

Encompassing hundreds of stops in Mississippi and neighboring states, the trail tells the story of multitudes of men and women, where and how they lived, and how they influenced the blues movement and music forever. Visiting these places helps you feel some of the trials and tribulations each faced in life.

Coastal Mississippi is very proud of the distinguished places included on the trail, from a blues radio station to a venue on the Chitlin' Circuit. Exploring these spots and reading the markers placed—learning the history—is truly fascinating. You will develop a whole new appreciation for our area and its influence on blues music.

msbluestrail.org/coast

TIP

Download the Mississippi Blues Trail app to your phone. Each time you visit a marker, check in on the app. You will also find a complete list of all the markers along the trail as well as a host of other valuable information.

DARE TO WIN
AT THE BEAU RIVAGE RESORT AND CASINO

As the only MGM property in Coastal Mississippi, the Beau Rivage Resort and Casino provides the utmost hospitality and luxury.

Offering glamour with all-encompassing views of the Mississippi Sound, the Beau has been called "Queen B." Renowned entertainers, as well as up-and-coming new artists, often perform here. Notable events in the showroom and high-end lounges offer a variety of choices for guests. Dining outlets in the resort present you with everything from American to Italian to Pan-Asian cuisine plus more casual experiences. At the casino you can play table games, slots, and sportsbook. The fantastic pool, spa, salon, and luxury shopping complete the experience. Weddings, conferences, and conventions all find the Beau offers them the splendor they are looking for to show their attendees.

You have access to Fallen Oak, an 18-hole, par 72 championship layout golf course, if you are a guest.

875 Beach Blvd., Biloxi, 888-750-7111
beaurivage.mgmresorts.com

31

CAPTURE SOME LUCK
AT THE IP CASINO RESORT AND SPA

As a past winner of the Best of Gaming on the Gulf Coast, the IP Casino Resort and Spa offers much. It can be your one-stop resort destination. You will find over 1,200 slots and table games for your enjoyment. How about sportsbook and poker to challenge your ability?

The 32-floor hotel has plush rooms offering guests the ultimate comfort with views of the Back Bay. Fine dining as well as casual options are available. Three lounges, a high-end wine and spirits bar, a sports bar, arcade, spa, and salon round out their amenities.

The showroom furnishes comedy shows, urban shows, and country and rock-music shows as entertainment for the resort's visitors and community. If golf is your game, the IP can get you access to some of the finest, most beautiful courses on the Coast.

There is fun for everyone!

850 Bayview Ave., Biloxi, 888-946-2847
ipbiloxi.com

32

ROCK ON
AT THE HARD ROCK HOTEL AND CASINO BILOXI

For many people, music is a key to good living. This means not only listening but learning about various musical talents. This love of music is why the Hard Rock brand is so successful, and here in Coastal Mississippi, we have our own Hard Rock Hotel and Casino Biloxi.

Here you can enjoy not only your favorite table games and slots but also immerse yourself in all music genres. One of the sensational amenities offered is Sound of Your Stay. What mood are you hoping to set for your visit? The Hard Rock offers you a personalized playlist.

Their tower rooms offer incredible views of the water. The spa and dining offerings add the finishing touches. The numerous lounges have entertainment nightly, and Hard Rock Live also brings in notable headliners.

So get the Led out and rock on!

777 Beach Blvd., Biloxi, 228-374-7625
hrhcbiloxi.com

CATCH SOME RAYS
AT THE GOLDEN NUGGET BILOXI

With the sunshine offered in the South, what's more relaxing than grabbing a cold beverage and heading to the sanctuary of a refreshing pool and lounging away a few hours? At the Golden Nugget Biloxi, you can do precisely that! Seize that deluxe daybed or private cabana and idle away the day.

Enjoy beautifully appointed rooms and a gaming floor right off the parking garage. You can shop and decide on your entertainment preference for the evening once you've played a little. Well-known restaurants such as Morton's The Steakhouse and Bubba Gump Shrimp Co. offer you delectable meals. Are you feeling like just a drink to watch the game or perhaps some Asian cuisine instead? They have that as well. In the morning, Starbucks will start your morning properly.

Treat yourself to a bit of relaxation and fun, all while enjoying the beauty of the area.

151 Beach Blvd., Biloxi, 228-435-5400
goldennugget.com/biloxi

INDULGE YOURSELF
AT THE SCARLET PEARL CASINO RESORT

While all the casino resorts in Coastal Mississippi offer slots and table games, the Scarlet Pearl Casino Resort offers a VIP experience unlike others by way of its Orchid Room. Here is a high-limit gaming adventure unlike any other. In the Orchid Room, guests enjoy private gaming, their own TV at the slots, and a phone charger, as well as private hosts and an exceptional cocktail service. Sportsbook, other table games, and slots are available on the regular gaming floor.

Hotel rooms are luxurious and offer lovely views of the Back Bay. One of the most incredible amenities available to guests is the Lava Links Golf Club—miniature golf at its best. You will meander through waterfalls, gardens, and a volcano with music as a backdrop for great family fun as you play the game.

Join in the fun at the Pearl.

9380 Central Ave., D'Iberville, 888-752-9772
scarletpearlcasino.com

GRAVITATE TO THE GREAT LAWN

AT HARRAH'S GULF COAST

What is the Great Lawn, one might ask? Let Harrah's Gulf Coast answer that question. The Great Lawn is an outdoor event venue sitting on the waterfront, encompassing over 10 acres. It has hosted some notable concerts in the area, such as Kenny Rogers, REO Speedwagon, Toby Keith, and Collective Soul, to name only a few. It is a festival green space, wide open with no seating assigned. It is general admission only and pit-style; most bring blankets and lawn chairs.

If golfing is your game, Harrah's has its own Jack Nicklaus–designed 18-hole course to lure you, widely considered one of the best on the Coast.

Your hotel stay will give you all-new in-room entertainment. The gaming floor offers tables and slots, as well as sportsbook. Enjoy dining options from fine to casual. A spa, salon, and pool will enhance your efforts at relaxation.

Have some fun!

280 Beach Blvd., Biloxi, 800-946-2946
caesars.com/harrahs-gulf-coast

36

WATCH THE SPARKLING WATER

AT ISLAND VIEW CASINO AND BEACH VIEW HOTEL

As Gulfport's only casino, Island View Casino Resort now has not only one but two casino resort hotels. Island View Hotel is the first and offers a myriad of amenities for your pleasure. Beach View Hotel is the newest and is a smoke-free environment. Both hotels provide brilliant views of the Gulf waters.

Gaming is available at both locations, as is sportsbook. Dining experiences abound, from casual to steakhouses and daiquiri bars. Each hotel offers live music at its late-night bars. The Buffet is well known for serving some of the best food for breakfast, lunch, dinner, and Sunday brunch.

The 18-hole Windance is one of America's best championship courses. Recently renovated, it provides Island View golfing guests the opportunity to play one of the top courses in Mississippi.

Check out what Island View and Beach View have to offer.

3300 W Beach Blvd., Gulfport, 228-314-2100
islandviewcasino.com

ENJOY A HOMEY ATMOSPHERE
AT THE SILVER SLIPPER

Are you looking for a bit more laid-back casino experience? "Come on down to the Silver Slipper" is their tagline, and it works. The Silver Slipper has become a perfect choice for many residents and visitors from close-by Louisiana, as it has much to offer.

Their hotel rooms afford a splendid view of the gorgeous Gulf of Mexico. Slots, table games, sportsbook, and keno are available. So is high-limit gaming. Multiple dining options, including a buffet and beach bar, give guests compelling ways to relax. Many nights, folks find live entertainment at the Stage Bar.

Do you already have your traveling accommodations but still want to stay a few days? No problem. The Silver Slipper has an RV park directly on the beach. Park, snap a few pictures of the beautiful area, and come on inside.

5000 S Beach Blvd., Bay St. Louis, 228-469-2777
silverslipper-ms.com

38

VENTURE INTO THE OLD WEST
AT BOOMTOWN CASINO BILOXI

Boomtown Casino Biloxi is the "Original Locals Casino." With its Western-inspired theme as décor, you will find a unique setting for your gaming experience. In Boomtown, you will find a poker room, slots, sportsbook, and table games in some of the friendliest surroundings. Southern hospitality thrives here. On Saturdays, entertainment is generally offered right on the gaming floor.

Fat Tuesday at Boomtown Daiquiri is located away from the casino in downtown Biloxi. Here you will find a New Orleans–style bar with an outdoor patio, indoor and outdoor TVs to watch your favorites, and some of the best daiquiri concoctions in town. Boomtown's dining choices consist of Asian fusion and a sports bar and grill.

Boomtown does not have a hotel, but there is an RV park directly across the street to accommodate those traveling through the area.

Perhaps you'll strike gold in the Old West.

676 Bayview Ave., Biloxi, 228-435-7000
boomtownbiloxi.com

39

BOOST YOUR MOOD
AT TREASURE BAY CASINO AND HOTEL

A mixture of Southern charm, comfort, and elegance greets the guests of Treasure Bay Casino and Hotel.

Whether you are in town for business or pleasure, here you can find the relaxation and contentment you are looking for. From your balcony, you'll have a view either of the Gulf waters or the pool deck. No matter: take a deep breath and enjoy.

Choose to refresh yourself in the company of friends at Blu, the chic lounge within Treasure Bay. Dine on delicious offerings like crab legs—for lunch or dinner! You can also try an outstanding shrimp and crawfish pasta, all next to the vast full-length windows with a view of the water. Table games, sportsbook, and slots—including new games—are available for your pleasure. Whatever you choose will be well worth it and help make your visit memorable.

Revel in the moment.

1980 Beach Blvd., Biloxi, 228-385-6000
treasurebay.com

40

FLOAT ON A LAZY RIVER
AT THE HOLLYWOOD CASINO GULF COAST

Doesn't floating along on a 350-foot lazy river sound appealing? At the Hollywood Casino Gulf Coast, you can do just that and so much more. And when you've completed this bout of relaxation, you can walk a few steps to your room or the gaming floor.

At Hollywood, you will find a full array of Las Vegas–style gaming: slots, poker, table games, and sportsbook. You can then move on to Bogart's Steakhouse, where award-winning chefs will prepare an exceptional meal for you. There is also a buffet and a couple of grill restaurants. Bogart's is only one of the dining options.

If golf is your preference, enjoy an Arnold Palmer signature course during your visit. Hollywood is accessible by boat, and they have their marina where patrons can dock and join in the fun. An RV park is also available.

Relish the experience at Hollywood.

711 Hollywood Blvd., Bay St. Louis, 866-758-2591
hollywoodgulfcoast.com

FEEL THE EXCITEMENT
AT PALACE CASINO RESORT

Palace Casino Resort is the only smoke-free casino in Biloxi and was redesigned to offer an exceptional comfort level to the guest experience.

Coastal images taken by local photographers adorn this resort's deluxe accommodations. Casino action here is exciting, offering slots, table games, and sports betting. Mississippi lottery tickets are also available here. Dining options are varied. From Mignon's Steaks and Seafood to the Palace Buffet to the Stacked Grill, visitors will find something appealing to their taste buds. Ready to relax? Try a massage or facial at the spa. Ready to tee off? Play a round of golf at a Jerry Pate–designed course.

During the temperate months of the year, Wahoo's Poolside Bar & Grill is open. Dock your boat, hop off, and have one of the best Bushwhackers available on the Coast. Just be sure not to drink and boat!

158 Howard Ave., Biloxi, 228-432-8888
palacecasinoresort.com

Mississippi Aquarium

SPORTS AND RECREATION

42

HOP ON BOARD
THE TWISTED TIKI BAR BOAT CRUISES

Are you looking for a unique, funky way to enjoy the water? If taking a trip on a boat decorated and themed for the island life sounds fun, then jump on board the Twisted Tiki Bar Boat Cruises. The cruise is a fun way to spend a couple of hours on the water.

Several options are available: sightseeing, sunset, after-hours, or a mimosa tiki cruise. One can even rent the Tiki Boat for a private event. They have adult beverages and snacks for purchase as well as fabulous music. As a bonus, the crew is friendly and engaging, reminiscent of an island tiki bar on land—this one just floats.

Try the sunset cruise where an impromptu dance party could very well break out. Cruising on the water with the sunset as your backdrop and terrific tunes that set the mood—it's the best! What more could you ask for?

100 Joy Compretta Dr., Bay St. Louis, 228-304-2611
twistedtikitours.com

TIP

If you would like to experience a cruise on an old-time paddle boat, check out the availability of their sister cruise—The *Betsy Ann Riverboat*. Try the historical and ecological tour or the popular hibachi dinner cruise. These cruises can be found on their website too.

43

LEARN ABOUT WORKING THE SEA

ON THE BILOXI SHRIMPING TOUR

Have you ever enjoyed a fabulous seafood dinner and wondered about what goes into the process of procuring those tasty tidbits?

Climb aboard the Biloxi Shrimping Tour to find out. You receive valuable insight and information on the nuances of the shrimping and fishing industry. You also are highly entertained. The captain and crew on board are genuinely engaging and knowledgeable about this fickle industry. You will learn how weather and pollution directly relate to the bounty of the sea. You will learn about salinity and water temperature and how it affects everything that makes its home in the water.

The net will trawl behind the boat and bring in a sampling of shrimp, crabs, and fish. The seagulls will trail behind you, hoping for any tidbits you may offer them. All ages will truly enjoy this nearly 90-minute trip out through the water.

693 Beach Blvd., Biloxi, 228-392-8645
biloxishrimpingtrip.com

WALK THE BEACH HAND IN HAND
TO ENJOY THE COAST

With 62 miles of coastline and 26 miles of beach access, there is always a place to enjoy the ever-changing personality of the Mississippi Sound, the estuary that is off our coastline leading to the beautiful Gulf of Mexico. Some days it will be smooth as silk, another day, the sun will sparkle on the water like diamonds, and yet another day, it may look angry and upset when the weather is approaching our coast.

We have many piers and walkways where visitors and residents can take a pleasant stroll and enjoy the fresh air. Bicycles are also a regular sight. One of the newest walking opportunities is West Biloxi Boardwalk. This is being built in phases and connects beachside restaurants and attractions while allowing a stunning view of the water. If you feel the need to get your feet wet, go for it! The scenery makes getting a bit of exercise fun.

gulfcoastorg.com
biloxi.ms.us

45

GAZE UPON COOL CREATURES
AT THE MISSISSIPPI AQUARIUM

One of our newest attractions, the Mississippi Aquarium brings to life many local marine creatures while also focusing on the importance of education and conservation.

When you make your way to the top floor, you'll find an open display where you can touch crabs, stingrays, shrimp, and an albino shark. Once you have seen all the creatures in the holding tank, walk down a spiral walkway encircling the main attraction. This tank contains over one million gallons of water and legions of sea creatures. The design is spectacular and gives so many opportunities to view marine life.

You will experience dolphins, alligators, otters, and even an aviary in the outdoor exhibits. Many of the displays also teach visitors about conservation. The aquarium and all its information will help you discover the bounty of the water and the area's ecosystem.

2100 E Beach Blvd., Gulfport, 228-241-1300
msaquarium.org

TIP

Become an annual member. Being a member gains you access to special benefits such as exclusive events and presentations (such as a breakfast and learning more about dolphin research). Also, any guests you bring receive a discount on their admission cost.

46

KAYAK, EXPLORE, AND LEARN
AT THE PASCAGOULA RIVER AUDUBON CENTER

Are you looking to while away a few hours immersed in nature outdoors? The Pascagoula River Audubon Center is the place to be.

Stroll the grounds of this remarkable place tucked away along the Pascagoula River, the longest free-flowing river in the lower 48 states. Experience one of the most unique ecosystems in the country. As you explore the grounds and nature center, you will see and learn so much about the local flora and fauna of the area. A great time to visit is during the Hummingbird Festival.

Rent a kayak or bring your own. Nothing surpasses being on the river and seeing ospreys, eagles, cormorants, and snowy egrets, just to name a few birds here. Venture into the inlets, and you are liable to catch the eyes of a gator in the marshes. Be cautious but enjoy nature all around.

5107 Arthur St., Moss Point, 228-475-0825
pascagoula.audubon.org

ENJOY RARE BIRD-WATCHING

AT THE MISSISSIPPI SANDHILL CRANE REFUGE

Imagine the only place in the world, in the wild, where you can see a precious endangered species. That place is the Mississippi Sandhill Crane Refuge. The sandhill crane is critically endangered, with only approximately 110 left in the world. The refuge is here to help preserve the habitat needed for this crane species to live. You may also see several other birds that find the sanctuary a haven, such as the Henslow's sparrow, prothonotary warbler, or the bald eagle.

Hike through the wet pine savannah habitat and see cypress trees in all their glory. Check out the carnivorous plants and beautiful orchids. Be sure to also pick up the checklists inside the visitor center. This way you can keep a record of all that you see! Using these checklists, with all the photo opportunities you will likely encounter, will provide you with memories long after you depart.

7200 Crane Ln., Gautier, 228-497-6322
fws.gov/refuge/mississippi_sandhill_crane

PLAY WITH DOLPHINS

AT THE INSTITUTE OF MARINE MAMMALS STUDIES AND OCEAN ADVENTURES MARINE PARK

Marine care is critical with our proximity to the Gulf of Mexico. Education as well as rescues are fundamental to the region, as are fun and enjoyment. You have it all between the Institute of Marine Mammals Studies (IMMS) and Ocean Adventures Marine Park.

IMMS cares for and treats many sea creatures that sadly become stranded on our beaches. Almost weekly, they rescue and rehabilitate sea turtles, dolphins, and other marine mammals. They provide education and summer camps to fill young minds and perhaps foster future career paths.

On the entertaining side of things, there is Ocean Adventures Marine Park. Bring the kids, bring the family, or come for an excursion on your own. Here you can interact and play with dolphins, get a kiss from a sea lion, or swim with the stingrays. How cool is that?

10801 Dolphin Ln., Gulfport, 228-896-9182
imms.org
oceanadventures.us

PLY THE WAVES
ON THE BILOXI SCHOONER SAIL

Have you ever wanted to experience life in the age of glorious sailing ships? Well, with the Biloxi Schooner Sail, here is your chance. Come sail away on one of the beautiful and graceful "White Winged Queens." These two schooners offer day sails or private charter trips. The ships are replicas of the beautiful oyster schooners that sailed in Biloxi's waters from the late 1800s to the early 1900s. With the introduction of marine engines, they became obsolete.

There is something so serene in being on the water, hearing the song of the winds filling the sails and steering you to your destination.

Wouldn't this be an excellent one-of-a-kind way to celebrate a birthday, anniversary, or even a wedding? The *Glenn L. Swetman* and the *George Sekul* are elegant, beautiful vessels that will take you sailing and give you great enjoyment. They are part of the Maritime & Seafood Industry Museum.

367 Beach Blvd., Biloxi, 228-435-6320
maritimemuseum.org/new/biloxi-schooners

50

GET CLOSE TO BIG REPTILES
AT THE GULF COAST GATOR RANCH

Alligators are like prehistoric creatures, fascinating yet deadly in some circumstances. While not everyone wants to hold one, most like to look from afar. The Gulf Coast Gator Ranch provides that opportunity.

Do you want to tell others you've fed a gator up close and personal? Well, you can do so yet still protect yourself along the walkways through the ranch. Bring your camera because you will see some mighty large gators lounging about in the sun, soaking up the heat. The ranch allows you to hold the tiny ones, with their jaws secured, of course.

Take the airboat tour to see the alligators in their natural habitat, back through the bayous. You will likely also get a glimpse of birds and other marine life, providing they haven't become a meal for one of the elusive big reptiles. Beware—the airboat is loud by design, but it is a great experience to behold. Just keep your hands to yourself!

10300 US 90, Moss Point, 228-475-6026
airboatswamptoursofmississippi.com

ABSORB THE COAST'S SIGHTS AND SOUNDS

AT DAVIS BAYOU

Part of the Gulf Islands National Seashore, Davis Bayou has compelling natural beauty for the visitor and locals alike. There always seems to be something new with each visit.

Inside the visitor center are displays and exhibits about the Barrier Islands. Wander about and enjoy these areas of information. If you decide you'd like to drop a line, there is a fishing pier. There is no shop of any kind, so be sure to bring your equipment. Hiking trails abound, not long or arduous, but a nice walk. You will see native plants and trees on the hike and maybe a critter or two scurrying from the path. There will be birds galore, from ospreys and eagles to egrets or a pelican.

Launch your boat if you'd like or stay in the campground. Bring a picnic basket and enjoy your meal surrounded by the sights and sounds of nature.

3500 Park Rd., Ocean Springs, 228-230-4136
nps.gov/guis/planyourvisit/davis-bayou-area

SEE THE BEST BEACH
WITH SHIP ISLAND EXCURSIONS

Approximately 12 miles offshore is an island, only accessible by boat. Unless you own a watercraft, you'll want to head to Ship Island Excursions. Here you will secure a ferry ride to quite simply the most stunning beaches in the area. Once you travel over the Mississippi Sound, you will arrive at West Ship Island's beautiful blue-green waters and white sands.

The summer waters are fabulously warm, and the sky is crystal blue. When you swim in the waters, be sure to keep a close eye out for stingrays, crabs, and even some skittish small sharks. Perhaps like me, you'll have a school of small minnows circling you, avoiding larger predators. Walk all around, experience the shorebirds and look out over the vastness of the water. You won't be disappointed. Be sure to keep your sandals on—the sand is hot!

Ship Island Excursions offers other cruises as well. Check them out!

1040 23rd Ave., Gulfport, 228-864-1014
msshipisland.com

53

FLY PAST THE TREETOPS, LITERALLY,
AT ZIP N FUN

Have you ever imagined yourself as being Tarzan, King of the Jungle? At Zip N Fun, you can become a version of him if you so choose.

The adventures that thrive at Zip N Fun are for various ages. Two courses, either the regular treetop adventure or the junior adventure course, await you. Each of these offers an aerial ropes course and games. The farther you go along the route, the more ambitious it becomes. There are sky bridges and ziplines. At some point, if you stay on track, you will come upon the jump that will have you become your version of Tarzan. Will you master the jungle cry?

When you zip here, there, and everywhere, enjoy a great time with your family and friends. It is the only adventure like this on the Gulf Coast. You won't want to miss out on the fun.

17200 16th St., Gulfport, 228-206-7056
zipnfun.com

PICK UP SPOOKY LORE
ON THE MYSTIC GHOST BOAT AND WALKING TOUR

Ghost hunting is not just for Halloween! On the Mystic Ghost Boat and Walking Tour, when you venture onto the Ghost Boat to cruise the waters of Bayou Caddy, the spirits of old will surround you. Through the low-hanging branches of the trees to the mystical twists and turns of the bayou, Mystic Molly, a wonderful storyteller, will entertain you with tales from the mysterious past. She will impart local lore to her passengers as you float across the water on the pontoon boat. Stay open-minded and feel the spirits around you.

Also offered in conjunction with the Ghost Boat is a walking tour of Old Town Bay St. Louis. The evening walk, beginning at a local watering hole, will take you through the dark streets, past haunted buildings, and through the cemetery in town. You will again hear of legends and known, documented sightings of paranormal activity in the area. So, go ahead and book a tour if you dare!

6149 Central Ave., Bay St. Louis, 228-363-9533
mysticghostrides.com

SPLASH THE DAY AWAY
AT GULF ISLANDS WATERPARK

Who doesn't love the fun and memories made at a water park? In the heat of the summer, Gulf Islands Waterpark is a haven where you can frolic with your entire family.

A word of advice: plan for your visit. If you are spending the day and want to be sure you have a private place to rest in the shade, go ahead and rent a cabana or pavilion. These cool hangouts rent extremely fast! Water slides of varying intensities are available for these fun times.

If you're only here with us briefly, consider stopping by for a day. Frequent visitors and residents find great value in buying the season passes, available each year. Think of what a great gift these passes could be for a friend or loved one! Whenever the mood strikes, off they go. Don't forget the sunblock!

17200 16th St., Gulfport, 228-328-1266
gulfislandswaterpark.com

ROOT
FOR BILOXI SHUCKERS BASEBALL

Minor-league baseball made a resurgence in the area back in 2015. The Biloxi Shuckers became the hometown team, bringing together a local fan base. They are a Double-A affiliate for the Milwaukee Brewers.

The Shuckers' home field is MGM Park in downtown Biloxi, beautifully situated with 4,500 reserved seats, suites, open-air party decks, a terrace, and a luxury club. You get a wide variety of ticket options, from season tickets to individual tickets, making it affordable for all. MGM Park holds select special events in the off-season.

Perhaps you've heard of major-league baseball player Barry Lyons. Barry is a Biloxi native and worked tirelessly to secure baseball's return to his hometown. He is now the Shuckers' Team Ambassador, promoting them at every opportunity. Join him and come on out to enjoy a game!

105 Caillavet St., Biloxi, 228-233-3465
milb.com/biloxi

57

CHEER
FOR MISSISSIPPI SEAWOLVES HOCKEY

For the first time in many years, as of Fall 2022, professional hockey has returned to Coastal Mississippi. The Mississippi Seawolves' home rink is in Biloxi at the Mississippi Coast Coliseum.

One might think hockey in a warm climate is a bit odd. Thousands of fans at three recent exhibition games proved that wrong. Hockey's resurrection in Coastal Mississippi brings another form of sporting entertainment to our area.

The final approval and details for the team are happening as of this writing. We know the team will be closely connected to the community and expand their already loyal following. Fans made their voices known with their support, and everyone listened.

Stay tuned by checking for updates on the team's website.

228-999-8333
mississippiseawolves.com

58

GLIDE OVER THE WATER
ON SAILING CHARTERS

When in a coastal destination, it would be a shame not to take advantage of the glorious water and the fun and relaxation it offers. Why not venture out on a sailing excursion? Maybe even have a chance to explore all the Barrier Islands off our shore.

There are numerous sailing charters available for you to experience. Some may even offer lessons, and the next thing you know, you'll be purchasing your little Sunfish and captaining it yourself! What better way to savor the simple beauty around you?

Enjoy the coastal waters! Listed here are only a few of the companies that offer sailing charters. Do research, check them out, and make that call.

North Star Sailing Charters
2250 Jones Park, Gulfport, 228-617-8057
northstarsailingcharters.com

Adventure Charters
679 Beach Blvd., Biloxi, 228-380-0471
adventure-charters.com

Island Hopper Charters
Pass Christian Harbor, Pass Christian
228-224-5432
islandhopperchartersllc.com

CATCH THE BIG ONE
ON FUN FISHING CHARTERS

As Biloxi was once known as the seafood capital of the world, fishing is in our blood here in Coastal Mississippi.

Areas to fish are abundant—both salt water and fresh water. There are over 200 different species of fish waiting to challenge you to bring them in. People fish from shore, off piers, and from multitudes of boats that dot the horizon on any given day.

Are you looking for more of a challenge? Do you want to go deep-sea fishing? Perhaps you don't have a boat available to you that will take you into the deeper waters of the Gulf. Never fear. We have you covered.

With well over 50 different fishing-boat charter options, your ultimate choice will depend on the season, the catch you are after, your budget, and your ability level. Nearly every city along the coast has options, so take your pick and get out there and enjoy!

gulfcoast.org/things-to-do/fishing

MAKE PLAYING IN THE WATER BETTER
WITH BEACH RENTALS

You long to go to the beach and have some fun playing in the water—what to do? Several places along the coast allow you to secure rentals for all you need to enjoy your day. You can rent and reserve a picnic table and an umbrella and chairs. Want the thrill of zipping through the Mississippi Sound? Try renting a Jet Ski. There is an abundance of toys you can acquire for the day. Maybe a kayak or paddleboard. Perhaps an aqua cycle. You can even get your hands on a Polaris slingshot, moped, scoot coupe, or bicycle. There are so many ways to enjoy the 26 miles of beach in front of you. Which will you choose?

Biloxi Beach Jet Ski Rentals
2640 Beach Blvd., Biloxi, 228-297-5647
facebook.com/biloxibeachjetskirentals

Life's a Beach Rental
1617 Beach Blvd., Biloxi, 228-697-5176
facebook.com/lyfesabeach2017

Get Wet, Inc.
2428 Beach Blvd., Biloxi, 228-806-4372
jetskibiloxi.com

61

SWING THOSE CLUBS
AT AWESOME GOLF DESTINATIONS

Whether you are an avid golfer or just a novice, Coastal Mississippi has a course that will suit not just your needs but your budget as well. Throw in fabulous views, a temperate climate, and golf courses designed by some great names, and you've got yourself the ultimate in the sport of golf. You've heard of Jack Nicklaus, Arnold Palmer, and Jerry Pate, right? These gentlemen, as well as several others, have designed some of our courses.

PGA and private tournaments flourish in our area because we have so many great courses to choose from. Many hotels and casinos have packages that visitors can purchase to make the most of their time here. Which will be your choice?

gulfcoast.org/things-to-do/golf

Windance Country Club
Gulfport, 228-832-4871
windancecc.com

Shell Landing
Gautier, 228-497-5683
shelllanding.com

The Preserve Golf Club
Vancleave, 228-386-2500
preservegc.com

Hickory Hill Country Club
Gautier, 228-497-2372
hickoryhillcc.com

Diamondhead Country Club
Diamondhead, 228-255-3910
diamondheadms.org

Sunkist Country Club
Biloxi, 228-388-3961
sunkistcc.com

Grand Bear Golf Club
Saucier, 228-265-9363
grandbeargolf.com

The Bridges
Bay St. Louis, 228-463-4047
hollywoodgulfcoast.com

Angel Tree

CULTURE AND HISTORY

EXPLORE
19TH-CENTURY FORT MASSACHUSETTS

Ship Island is a barrier island off the coast of Mississippi. Part of the Gulf Islands National Seashore, it is home to the historic Fort Massachusetts. The island is only accessible by water, either from a private boat or ferry service from the coast.

Built after the War of 1812, Fort Massachusetts had a prominent role in the Civil War. At one time, it was used as a POW camp and then eventually became the home of what would become the 2nd Louisiana Native Guards. As you tour the fort, the lurking sense of isolation felt by the soldiers is tangible.

The granite spiral staircases are eerie in their beauty. They take you to the top level, where you can see an entire cannon of the time. Be sure to be on the lookout for the elusive ghost crab scampering around the fort. It is pure white and quite intriguing.

West Ship Island, off the shore of Gulfport
nps.gov/guis/learn/historyculture/fort-massachusetts.htm

FINE-TUNE YOUR AESTHETIC SENSE

AT THE OHR-O'KEEFE MUSEUM OF ART

Have you ever heard of the "Mad Potter of Biloxi"? This fascinating man was George Ohr, a native of Coastal Mississippi. While he created over 7,000 personal pieces, he never received great recognition until after his death. The Ohr-O'Keefe Museum of Art is dedicated to his beautiful ceramic art and showcases much of his work.

In addition to his works, there are several contemporary and historical exhibitions from kindred artists. Exhibits do change, so there is always something new and exciting to see. The museum is also home to a ceramics studio that offers space to artists and classes on pottery for the novice.

The museum buildings, designed by renowned artist and architect Frank Gehry, are set among majestic live oaks with waters of the Gulf as a backdrop. The bold arrangement of five distinct buildings offers a separate, yet not isolated, experience for the visitors to the museum.

386 Beach Blvd., Biloxi, 228-374-5547
georgeohr.org

GET TO KNOW A LOCAL GENIUS
AT THE WALTER ANDERSON MUSEUM OF ART

While alive, Walter Anderson avoided the spotlight. He was somewhat of a hermit. He did not paint for fame but rather for himself. His life and work story is riveting, and visitors can learn everything about him at the Walter Anderson Museum of Art.

Mr. Anderson used a range of media for his art, whatever he could get. Sometimes it was wood. Other times it was canvas. He even at times used linoleum scraps or the back of wallpaper.

His genius is evident in the incomparable paintings, murals, drawings, sculptures, and other works of art housed in the museum. In the Ocean Springs's community center, attached to the museum, you will find a room where all the walls are mural paintings done by Mr. Anderson detailing the city's history. The beauty and detail are astounding.

The intensity of Mr. Anderson's focus on coastal plants, animals, landscapes, and people means his art is highly sought after by collectors.

510 Washington Ave., Ocean Springs, 228-872-3164
walterandersonmuseum.org

CHANNEL YOUR INNER SCIENTIST
AT THE INFINITY SCIENCE CENTER AND NASA STENNIS VISITOR CENTER

Have you ever seen an honest-to-goodness rocket booster up close and personal? It is one enormous piece of equipment!

You will see that rocket and so much more at the INFINITY Science Center and NASA Stennis Visitor Center. The Saturn V rocket used by NASA's Apollo program for moon exploration—think Neil Armstrong. The piece on display at INFINITY was built for Apollo 19 and was one of several pieces left over after the Apollo program ended. It will leave you in awe!

There are numerous other fascinating displays at INFINITY. Another favorite is the 150-year-old pirogue (one-person wooden craft) from the Pearl River, dating well before there even was a NASA. Lose yourself in the native plant area, see a tarantula, and make a hurricane. You will learn things without even realizing it. Great for kids and adults alike!

1 Discovery Cir., Pearlington, 228-533-9025
visitinfinity.com

STAY AT A RESORT WITH HISTORY

AT CENTENNIAL PLAZA

When you turn onto the drive that brings you into Centennial Plaza, you will encounter a fabulous dancing fountain with color-changing jets choreographed to music. That's just the beginning.

The resort is on the site of Mississippi's 100th birthday commemoration in 1917. This celebration of Mississippi entering the Union faded quickly due to global war and a flu pandemic. The building and land became a place for military training and in later years the Veterans Administration Medical Center in Gulfport.

Centennial Plaza has two hotels and other renovated buildings, along with the fountain mentioned above. Under the beauty of dignified live oak trees, enjoy the serene pond and walking areas throughout the property. Your picture of simple beauty is complete.

This resort is a definite must-see.

200 E Beach Blvd., Gulfport, 228-206-7880
centennialplazams.com

67

LET THE GOOD TIMES ROLL AT THE COASTAL MISSISSIPPI MARDI GRAS MUSEUM

Mardi Gras is often associated with our neighboring city of New Orleans. But be assured, in Coastal Mississippi, it's a big deal! There are parades where you will hear voices sing, "Throw me something, Mister." There are elaborate balls with festival royalty in their fine costumes and traditions.

Do you want to learn what it's all about? Wander through the Coastal Mississippi Mardi Gras Museum in Biloxi. Here you will glimpse the history, passion, and magic of Mardi Gras. The costumes of previous kings, queens, and courts have been donated to be on display. You will see the intricacy of the designs and realize the effort and commitment it takes to be a part of the Krewe. You will read the history of how Mardi Gras became the holiday it is today. There is even a room to put on some of the costumes. Have some fun and learn at the same time!

LAISSEZ LE BON TEMPS ROULER!

792A Howard Ave., Biloxi, 228-314-4747
coastalmardigras.com

TRAVEL BACK IN TIME
AT BEAUVOIR, THE JEFFERSON DAVIS HOME AND PRESIDENTIAL LIBRARY

The Civil War was a time of a divided country and eventually the end to a way of life in the South. The history of that time runs deep. Beauvoir, the Jefferson Davis Home and Presidential Library, is a museum to visit and respect that bygone era and realize its importance in who we are today.

Jefferson Davis was the only president of the Confederacy, and Beauvoir was his last home. On its grounds, you will find the beauty of the Old South in an antebellum home facing the water, a memorial cemetery, a tomb for the Unknown Confederate Soldier, and a presidential library full of memorabilia and artifacts. The library houses a comprehensive collection of books and research material on the Confederacy and the Civil War, including a section where you can delve into genealogy and soldier records of the time.

2244 Beach Blvd., Biloxi, 228-388-4400
visitbeauvoir.org

LEARN OUR SEAFARING HERITAGE
AT THE MARITIME & SEAFOOD MUSEUM

Coastal Mississippi has a long maritime history, and the seafood industry is an integral part of our economy. To honor those facts, the Maritime & Seafood Museum was born. Within these walls reside 300 years of "history, heritage, and culture" of the seafaring life and how it sculpted the area and its residents.

The building itself is impressive, with a wall of windows facing the water. In this atrium stands the *Nydia*, fully masted, visible, and enticing you to hurry in and see her in all her glory. Other delightful exhibits include the wooden boat gallery, the Biloxi seafood factory gallery, and the commercial fishing gallery.

Give yourself plenty of time to stroll through all the exhibits, as there are many. The museum is multi-level and holds an abundance of information. It will give you an understanding of how deeply the maritime and seafood worlds intertwine with the history of this area.

1151 1st St., Biloxi, 228-456-6320
maritimemuseum.org

TOWER ABOVE IT ALL
AT THE BILOXI LIGHTHOUSE

Likely the most photographed landmark along our coast is the Biloxi Lighthouse. Constructed in 1848, it was one of the first lighthouses in the South, among three authorized for the Mississippi Sound by legislation sponsored by none other than the area's US representative in Congress at the time, Jefferson Davis.

As it stands regally over the water, the 64-foot cast-iron lighthouse is a truly magnificent sight. Located in the middle of what is now Highway 90, it reminds everyone of the strength and fortitude of Coastal Mississippi.

Hurricane Katrina's surge surrounded one-third of the lighthouse, breaking many windows and destroying some of the brick interiors of the structure. It was renovated and reopened in 2010. The historic landmark has prevailed against Katrina and many other storms. It still stands tall in all its glory and is a beacon of hope and perseverance. Anyone can venture to the top on daily morning tours.

Median of US 90 at Porter Avenue, Biloxi
biloxi.ms.us/visitor-info/museums/lighthouse

SEE MUSEUMS AND MAYBE A GHOST
AT THE L & N HISTORIC TRAIN DEPOT

Once used as the center point of the film *This Property Is Condemned*, the L & N Historic Train Depot is a two-story mission-style building with many tales to tell. Local legend has the structure haunted by the Depot Man, an apparition of a man in a white linen suit who tips his hat to you and vanishes. It is fascinating to explore as it serves as home to the county tourism board, the Bay St. Louis Mardi Gras Museum, and the Alice Moseley Folk Art Museum.

Explore the Bay St. Louis Mardi Gras Museum, viewing elaborate costumes and Mardi Gras scenes and stories. The Alice Moseley Folk Art Museum honors Miss Alice, a self-taught artist who painted to help her cope while caring for a family member with Alzheimer's disease. Her art is poignant and lovely and well worth a visit while there. In Miss Alice's own words, "I try to tell a story of the past in everything I paint."

Bay St. Louis Historic L & N Train Depot
1928 Depot Way, Bay St. Louis, 228-463-9222
gulfcoast.org/listings/bay-st-louis-historic-l%26n-train-depot/3830

Bay St. Louis Mardi Gras Museum
gulfcoast.org/listings/bay-st-louis-mardi-gras-museum

Alice Moseley Folk Art & Antique Museum
228-467-9223
alicemoseley.com

TAKE IN A COOL VIEW
AT THE BILOXI VISITORS CENTER

Directly behind the iconic Biloxi Lighthouse stands the Biloxi Visitors Center. The structure, which opened in 2011, pays homage to the area's architectural heritage. This stunning center bears a striking resemblance to Dantzler House, an antebellum home with two-story porches, a grand staircase, and floor-to-ceiling windows. A notorious lady named Katrina destroyed that original house on the property.

The views from the balcony are indescribable and the perfect place to capture that Kodak moment. Inside, you can access all things Biloxi. A theater shows a continuous showing of the short film *We Are Biloxi*. Many other small exhibits, as well as a gift shop, are located inside. The upper floor also serves as a lovely event venue for small meetings or small weddings.

1050 Beach Blvd., Biloxi, 228-374-3105
biloxi.ms.us/visitor-info/museums/visitors-center

TIP

Visit the Hurricane Katrina Memorial at the Biloxi Town Green at 133 Main Street. Dedicated to all the lives lost on August 29, 2005, it is 12 feet high. It represents the height of the storm surge at the town green where the memorial stands.

FEEL NATURE'S POWER
AT THE FRIENDSHIP OAK AND ANGEL TREES

What's so fascinating about a tree, one might ask? The Friendship Oak is an empress among trees. It is a massive 500-year-old Southern live oak on the University of Southern Mississippi (USM or Southern Miss) campus. Registered with the Live Oak Society, the tree is 59 feet tall with a trunk diameter of 5.75 feet. The tree's crown covers approximately 16,000 square feet. The Friendship Oak has withstood many hurricanes, including the devastation from Camille and Katrina. Legend says any who enter the shade of its branches remain friends for life. Truly a worthy goal and fabulous sight to see.

While visiting the city of Bay St. Louis, be sure to seek out "Angels in the Bay." Hurricane Katrina destroyed many of the area's treasured live oaks, ripping them from the ground and scattering them about. Chainsaw sculptor Dayle K. Lewis transformed these battered pieces of wood into angel works of art. Throughout the city, you will see these carved angels. You will be awed by the artist's sheer talent and compassion upon the community. They are truly magnificent.

USM Campus, 730 Beach Blvd., Long Beach
gulfcoast.org/listings/friendship-oak-tree
gulfcoast.org/listings/angel-trees-of-bay-st-louis

TIP

While admiring the Angel Trees in Bay St. Louis, look for something extra—some trees have ladybugs carved into them. See if you can find them. Also, some of these trees are very near Our Lady of the Gulf Catholic Church, a stunning Romanesque church built in 1908.

74

JOURNEY THROUGH BLACK MUSIC HISTORY

AT 100 MEN HALL

Music history and Mississippi are irrevocably intertwined. Not only of the musical kind but African American history as well. Nowhere is this more evident than at 100 Men Hall. History vibrates from the walls of this small, unassuming building.

In the early twentieth century, African Americans could not assemble together. Segregation laws kept Black musicians to a narrow window of performance opportunities known as the Chitlin' Circuit. 100 Men Hall became a stop for these talented men and women. 100 Men Hall became a gathering place for meetings, social events, and other significant life events like weddings and funerals.

Musical greats such as Fats Domino, B. B. King, Etta James, Ray Charles, Chuck Berry, and James Brown—to name only a few—played on the stage that remains in the house. A visit here is a step back in time and truly captivating.

303 Union St., Bay St. Louis
the100menhall.com

LEARN ABOUT PILOT HEROES
AT THE MISSISSIPPI AVIATION HERITAGE MUSEUM

John C. Robinson was the first African American pilot to fight in combat. This fight took place against Mussolini in 1935–1936 during the Ethiopian war. Did you know that? The Mississippi Aviation Heritage Museum was born through the efforts of community leaders to honor the legacy of all those within the state who have had a significant contribution to aviation. Within this museum's walls, you will learn of Mr. Robinson and other great aviators and astronauts from Mississippi.

The Tuskegee Gallery is incredible, highlighting stories of the Tuskegee Airmen's accomplishments and struggles that pushed them to excellence as World War II fighter and bomber pilots. Another exceedingly exciting gallery talks of our own Hurricane Hunters, who fly from our local Keesler Air Force Base.

Many Mississippians helped forge history in the field of aviation. This museum shows appreciation for their efforts and bravery.

429 Pass Rd., Gulfport, 228-864-6359
msaviationmuseum.org

VENTURE BACK IN HISTORY

AT THE LAPOINTE-KREBS AND CHARNLEY-NORWOOD HOUSES

Imagine standing inside the oldest standing structure in the Mississippi Valley. You can do just that at LaPointe-Krebs House. Scientifically dated as being built in 1757, this structure predates the Revolutionary War. The construction of this building is the only example of its kind anywhere on the Gulf Coast. The museum at the house shows its rich history and sheds light on the varied people who have lived there.

Charnley-Norwood House, having been designed by famed architects Louis Sullivan and Frank Lloyd Wright in the style known as Prairie School, was built as a vacation home for a wealthy Chicago lumber mogul in 1890. Although heavily damaged during Hurricane Katrina, the building did survive. Some pieces of the house became caught up in the debris left behind. Volunteers collected these pieces, and eventually the building was restored and is now the only Frank Lloyd Wright house in Mississippi that is open for public view.

LaPointe-Krebs House
4602 Fort St., Pascagoula
228-471-5126
lapointekrebs.org

Charnley-Norwood House
509 E Beach Dr., Ocean Springs
228-234-7298

OTHER HISTORIC HOMES IN THE AREA

Bond Grant House
932 Howard Ave., Biloxi, 228-435-6339
mainstreetbiloxi.com

Kate Lobrano House
103 Cue St., Bay St. Louis, 228-467-4090
hancockcountyhistoricalsociety.com

Oak Crest Mansion Inn
5267 Menge Ave., Pass Christian, 228-452-5677
oakcrestmansion.com

Old Brick House
662 Bayview Ave., Biloxi, 228-452-6244
biloxi.ms.us

The Grand Magnolia
3604 Magnolia St., Pascagoula, 228-696-1894
grandmagnolia.com

The Redding House
770 Jackson St., Biloxi, 228-207-4276
thereddinghouse.com

SEE WHERE A LOCAL SODA BEGAN

AT BARQ'S POP FACTORY

As you enjoy Barq's root beer, know that it originated in Coastal Mississippi, in a humble house that remains standing.

Edward Barq Sr. moved to Biloxi in 1897 and produced and sold his unique flavored root beer. It quickly became a local favorite and a national one as well. The Prohibition era brought huge sales of root beer. This original building was able to sustain the production needs until 1937. The company then moved to a larger facility, not far from the original, to continue its growth.

Barq's continued to enjoy much success and is now under the corporate umbrella of Coca-Cola.

However, the history of its beginning remains rooted in this small building.

142 Keller Ave., Biloxi
discover.biloxi.ms.us/barqs-pop-factory

SHOW A CHILD HOW LEARNING CAN BE FUN

AT THE LYNN MEADOWS DISCOVERY CENTER

A couple blocks up from the beach, in a schoolhouse constructed in 1915, you will find one cool place for kids! Lynn Meadows Discovery Center opened in 1998 as the first children's museum in Mississippi. The philosophy of the museum is to make learning fun for kids using interactive displays and exhibits.

Here kids will find an indoor climbing structure and the Dolan Avenue Depot with props and costumes from a time when trains were all the rage. There are fun and exciting science exhibits. Outdoors under the oak trees, you will find Bear Street, On the Green, and Solar Sunflowers, just to name a few.

Camps, kids' classes in arts and cooking, science—the list goes on and on. Visiting here makes you wish you were a kid again! As the winner of several awards, Lynn Meadows operates with community spirit and the desire to help kids learn and appreciate.

246 Dolan Ave., Gulfport, 228-897-6039
lmdc.org

79

EXPAND YOUR CREATIVITY

AT THE MARY C. O'KEEFE CULTURAL ART CENTER

Have you wanted to explore your inner artist but are not sure how? Head over to the Mary C. O'Keefe Cultural Art Center, known locally as the Mary C. Here you will find a unique combination of arts-based education and community involvement.

What is your favorite art form? Ceramics? Music? Dance? Photography? The Mary C offers instruction classes for art in many forms. You will also be able to catch some great performances, lectures, and other events.

The historic building is a piece of art. There are mural tiles painted and fired by the famed Anderson family. Inside the Mary C are two art galleries that feature local artwork and the Ocean Springs Historical Museum. The performing-arts theater is a lovely spot to enjoy a concert or a play.

Let the artist in you enjoy all the Mary C has to offer.

1600 Government St., Ocean Springs, 228-875-6732
themaryc.art

ENTER A HOBBYIST'S DREAM AT THE MISSISSIPPI COAST MODEL TRAIN MUSEUM

Do you or someone you know have a fascination with model trains? How about LEGO building? At the Mississippi Coast Model Train Museum, you will find one of the largest LEGO railroad displays in Mississippi.

One display that will catch your eye immediately runs throughout the museum, through different rooms, overhead, and all around, with model trains. Through the museum, you will find many showcases housing hundreds of trains. It is truly remarkable. There are interactive displays where kids (and adults!) can operate the trains. The LEGO display is simply massive.

Outside, there is a track with a train you can ride. It takes you through the gardens, maybe even through Jurassic Park. Kids and adults will be fascinated by the train models and the sheer number of them on display. Right after Thanksgiving, they have a terrific Christmas light show and fun special-event nights at holiday time. Fun for the whole family.

504 Pass Rd., Gulfport, 228-284-5731, mcmrcm.org

CAMP IN AN OLD PIRATE'S LAIR
AT BUCCANEER STATE PARK

In the late 1700s, pirating and smuggling were prevalent in Coastal Mississippi. Perhaps you've heard the name Jean Lafitte. Some call him a French buccaneer. Others refer to him as simply a pirate. Either way, the land, which is now home to Buccaneer State Park, was once settled by Lafitte and his band of smugglers. The pirate himself lived in the Old Pirate House, just steps from where the state park now sits.

Andrew Jackson also once used the site as a military operations base during the Battle of New Orleans. He also built and lived in a house that is now part of the park. Nowadays, the site serves as a state park where people camp, swim, play, fish, hike, and golf in a beautiful setting. The oak trees, draped with Spanish moss, are the perfect backdrop to a place housing such rich history.

1150 S Beach Blvd., Waveland, 228-467-3822
mdwfp.com/parks-destinations/state-parks/buccaneer

Shearwater Pottery Mug

SHOPPING AND FASHION

82

ENCOURAGE THE LOVE OF READING
AT PASS CHRISTIAN BOOKS

Located in a two-story building in the charismatic city of Pass Christian, you will find Pass Books. Sharing this lovely space is Cat Island Coffeehouse. What better combination could there be? Grab a cup of Joe, head out onto the deck overlooking the Gulf of Mexico, and lose yourself in a great book.

Pass Books came out of the owners' pure love of books and reading. This love turned into a classic independent bookstore. Are you looking for work done by a Mississippi author? Look no further than the Mississippi Loft on the second floor.

Pass Books also promotes its passion for the value of reading in many forms. The store hosts multiple book-signing events, has an online store for the convenience of its clientele, and promotes a community reading project called "One Book One Pass." This program fosters community engagement in a particular book, and it works with the local school district to provide this book to students.

300 E Scenic Dr., Pass Christian, 228-222-4827
passbooksonline.com

TIP

At Cat Island Coffeehouse, you can not only get superb coffees and opulent teas, but tasty soups and other foods as well. So grab that book, a bite to eat, and enjoy the fantastic view. Fun fact: Cat Island was named such because explorers who discovered the island saw all the raccoons and thought they were cats.

EXPERIENCE HANDCRAFTED BEAUTY
AT HILLYER HOUSE

For over 50 years, Hillyer House "mermaids" have offered exceptional art pieces to visitors and residents alike.

After Hurricane Camille, Hillyer House started in the community spirit of offering help to those in need by providing a place to replenish necessities. It has turned into much more and now stands as a shop where you can find beautiful pottery, handmade jewelry, glass, and wearables crafted by local artists. The shop prides itself on working with some of the same folks for over 30 years.

Inside the store, you will find a breathtaking display of handblown glass rondels: circular, often irregular creations, each one totally unlike another. Created by local glassblower Jerry Spehr to celebrate the store's 50th year, this display is VISION. It is difficult to explain the outright beauty of VISION. Visiting is the best way to appreciate it and all the other treasures housed within.

920 Washington Ave., Ocean Springs, 228-875-8065
hillyerhouse.com

84

CATCH THE LOOK OF NEW ORLEANS

AT FLEURTY GIRL

Looking for a fantastic gift for yourself or someone you know? One that has the flavor of New Orleans but doesn't make you drive to the city? Fleurty Girl started with a dream of a native of New Orleans to make T-shirts and now has expanded to six storefronts and an online store.

Here you will find the unique and different. The owner envisioned starting with just T-shirts, but now also has mugs, funky jewelry, candies, books, and door hangers among its fun merchandise. If you need Mardi Gras-themed anything, look no further. Without a doubt, they will have something classic or something crazy and different. From a "Smells Like the Parade Route" candle to headbands, earrings, and shirts, Fleurty Girl will make sure you know that Mardi Gras is in the air. You'll find something memorable. This fun, sassy store is a great place to pick up gifts for all your people, even those hard-to-please ones!

216 Main St., Bay St. Louis, 228-344-3106
fleurtygirl.net

BOOST YOUR ART COLLECTION

AT REALIZATIONS, THE WALTER ANDERSON SHOP

Earlier, we talked about the genius that was Walter Anderson. He expressed his talent in so many ways and used many different media. His family runs Realizations, the Walter Anderson Shop, to ensure his art is accessible to more people. They offer extensive silk-screened block prints and clothing, textiles, and household goods—all display designs by Mr. Anderson.

The intriguing thing about the block prints is they are, in fact, reproductions of an Anderson painting. These are available in black and white on heavy-weight watercolor paper. You can also purchase painted prints. The painted ones are water colored by highly skilled local artists, lending a bit of themselves to the famed Anderson print. There is a myriad of these items available, all individual and unique in their own way. Own or give a piece of Walter Anderson!

1000B Washington Ave., Ocean Springs, 228-875-0503
walterandersonart.com

FIND A NEW FAVORITE SCENT
FROM WAVELAND CANDLE COMPANY

If you require more candles for your home, Waveland Candle Company will gladly fill that need for you. Handmade soy candles are their specialty, and let me tell you, they are lovely.

Soy candles burn longer and burn clean. Interesting fact: the candles made by Waveland Candle Company are soy lotion candles. That means that you can use them as a lotion to combat issues such as eczema and psoriasis. Dual purpose! Beyond the fact that the candles are made with 100% soybean oil, the fragrances are heavenly.

So many fragrances, so little time! Aromas such as Fresh Cut Grass or Grandma's Kitchen entice your sense of smell. Perhaps something more like Rain or Sun & Sand suits you. There is even something called Butt Naked or Monkey Farts, for the devilish imp in you.

1804 Nicholson Ave., Waveland, 228-220-4716
wavelandcandle.com

REVOLUTIONIZE PRESENTS

WITH FINDS FROM MARTIN MIAZZA GIFTS

Named "a Coastal treasure" by *Southern Living* magazine, Martin Miazza Gifts has been family owned and operated for over 50 years and houses some remarkable gifts.

Started by Dot and Martin Miazza and now run by their daughter Kennedy, this shop carries luxurious products such as Baccarat and Wedgewood. Also available are items you cannot find anywhere else, one of those being the Mississippi Christmas ornament, which Mr. Miazza originally designed. These dated ornaments were well received, so the line has grown to include other Southern states and is only available through this store. Another exclusive line is that of Mississippi Groceries. These products encompass a variety of spreads, jams, relishes, and mustard.

When you walk through the doors of this unassuming store, you will find beauty and elegance, along with excellent service and a smile!

1208 Pass Rd., Gulfport, 228-863-1252
martinmiazza.com

TIP

Their wedding registry is one of the Coast's best-known. If a wedding is in your future, you need to stop by.

IGNITE YOUR IMAGINATION
AT SOUTHERN BOUND BOOK SHOP

From a fond childhood memory of a grandmother sharing a love of reading and books, the idea for Southern Bound Book Shop began to form. The dream became a reality, one to be proud of, an independent bookstore. Inside these walls, you will find new releases and used books. Were you looking for a vintage or collectible book? Southern Bound Book Shop has a large selection of those. Come on in and peruse those shelves.

You can find all manner of neat items for yourself and others. Some available items are made from recycled and salvaged goods, showing creativity. In addition, the shop features an array of different gifts from local artists. Chances are you will find something for everyone, even that "I already have everything" person on your list.

4030 Suzanne Dr., D'Iberville, 228-424-7257
facebook.com/southernboundbookshop

BROWSE THE SHOPS
OF CENTURY HALL

What's the best way to highlight and give new life to a centuries-old building? Help it become a gathering place of sorts, a place for boutique shops and galleries to call home. The Shops of Century Hall do just that. Within the original wooden building, you will find three stories of some of the neatest shops around.

For example, Matter of Hattery is "upcycling at its best." Here unique hats are made from other discarded items to give them a new attitude. In a Pinch Gifts has a great selection of accessories, home décor, apparel, and skincare. Bay Life Gifts offers such items as lamps, glassware, knives, wedding gifts, and so much more. You never know what you'll discover! These are just a handful of the type of shops you will find at Century Hall. Fun fact: the locals say this building just may be haunted.

112 S 2nd St., Bay St. Louis, 504-858-8574
shopsofcenturyhall.com

BUY FOR THAT PERSON WITH EVERYTHING

AT THE OHR-O'KEEFE MUSEUM GIFT SHOP

The Ohr-O'Keefe Museum Gift Shop is one of Coastal Mississippi's gems, almost as impressive as the museum itself. Do you have that one person in your life who has everything, and you never know what to get? Perhaps that describes you as well. Odds are you will find something at the Museum Store.

While the store is relatively small, it is packed full of items you won't find anywhere else. There are simple everyday items such as mugs and bowls, as well as one-of-a-kind jewelry and vases. The recipient will cherish these gifts and allow the giver to show their desire to offer something thoughtful to family and friends. The collection of art books is terrific. My choice was a fabulous book about none other than George Ohr, the art potter himself.

386 Beach Blvd., Biloxi, 228-374-5547
georgeohr.org/museum-store

FIND THE PERFECT GIFT
AT POPPY'S

The 2.7-mile-long Biloxi Bay Bridge connects the cities of Biloxi and Ocean Springs. The artsy latter town boasts many charming shops beckoning to you. Exceedingly popular among them is Poppy's. Here you will find a place filled with local art, gourmet food items, and an array of gifts to satisfy your shopping cravings.

You can browse in their friendly, relaxed atmosphere and even taste-test some gourmet foods. Candles and jewelry are available. Down the aisle, you may see some wreaths or other door decorations. Farther down, you'll come upon more home décor items. Their selection changes with new arrivals often, so just because you shopped there once doesn't mean you can't go back! Join in the shopping fun, and you'll find something you or a friend can't live without.

922 Washington St., Ocean Springs, 228-872-8584
facebook.com/shoppoppys

GET INSIDE A PREDATOR'S MOUTH
AT SHARKHEADS

As you drive down Highway 90 heading east, you will come upon a 32-foot shark leading into a big pink building. Really, you will. Sharkheads is the champion of souvenir shops. Nowhere else will you be able to have your photo taken within the jaws of a shark, right before you buy some tchotchkes to take home to commemorate your visit to their signature beach building.

The store has been a staple on the Coast for over 40 years. Completely devastated and swept away by Hurricane Katrina, Sharkheads rebuilt and reopened to serve the area again. It has the largest selection of "Biloxi Beach" merchandise anywhere. There are hundreds upon hundreds of items available for your pleasure. Take the elevator up a couple of stories and lose yourself in souvenir shopping—you could quite possibly be there for hours. Don't leave without taking that iconic photo! You know you want to.

1703 Beach Blvd., Biloxi, 228-374-9800
sharkheads.com

93

DISPLAY THAT PAINTING RIGHT

THANKS TO NEGROTTO'S FRAME & ART

Once you purchase the perfect print or even original painting from your favorite artist, or perhaps one from a new artist you just discovered, you will want the ideal accompaniment. At Negrotto's Frame & Art, you will undoubtedly find precisely the frame you need to showcase the piece. Negrotto's is a custom framing gallery, and they have on staff the only Certified Picture Framer in the state of Mississippi.

Taking pride in their work, as they know art shines through creativity and the perfect frame, they will work with you and advise on the ideal one for your painting. They can also help with preserving and protecting your art.

Negrotto's also has pottery, sculptures, and sometimes even some handcrafted jewelry. And check out their in-store gallery featuring works from over 20 local artists. While you're there, perhaps you will find another piece to add to your collection.

9036A Carl Leggett Rd., Gulfport, 228-335-4345
negrottosgallery.com

LOSE YOURSELF IN A NOVEL FROM BAY BOOKS

In Old Town Bay St. Louis, you will encounter many intriguing and fun things. One of those places will be Bay Books. As one of the very few independent bookstores on the Coast, it fills the need to offer a large selection of both new and used books to visitors and residents alike.

You can always find something new and exciting here. Perhaps you need a card to accompany your gift—no problem. Not much seems to be done on original stationery anymore, but pick some up at Bay Books for a nice touch. Surprise someone with a handwritten letter on that stationery—won't that be a great touch?

Booksellers here are supportive and experienced and are more than willing to help you find just what you need while you're in the store.

131 Main St., Bay St. Louis, 228-463-2688
mybaybooks.com

95

BUY ONE-OF-A-KIND PIECES
AT SHEARWATER POTTERY

Another famous artist in Walter Anderson's family was Peter, who started Shearwater Pottery in 1928. His medium was clay, and with his natural gift, he began to make stunning pottery known for the host of glaze and glaze combinations administered to each piece.

When purchasing a piece from Shearwater, you will get beauty and everyday functionality in most works. That means the pottery should be used in your day-to-day life. The coffee mugs I own serve my morning brew with beauty every day.

Peter's children still own Shearwater. Three of them are active in the ongoing legacy of making pottery as their father did. The showroom on the Anderson compound is nothing short of amazing, and if you leave there without a piece for your very own, my hat goes off to you as you're a stronger person than I am!

102 Shearwater Dr., Ocean Springs, 228-875-7320
shearwaterpottery.com

96

IMMERSE YOURSELF IN LOVE AND SPLENDOR

AT ROBIN'S NEST IN THE PASS

You will be immediately surrounded by the atmosphere of love, kindness, and faith when you arrive at Robin's Nest in the Pass. This gallery gift shop features all things celebrating a gifted spirit.

Throughout the store, you will find extraordinary gifts. Some fabulous artisan jewelry designed by the Roberts women is available, as well as the Power Collection, which is merchandise "meant to uplift, inspire, and motivate." There are also books of artwork by other area talent, much of it using our coast as inspiration. Lotions, clothing, and home goods are also available. There are so many gorgeous items you will be hard-pressed to choose between favorites.

As Robin Roberts's family owns this shop in their hometown of Pass Christian, you never know when she'll be in town picking up her favorites. Maybe you'll bump into her!

255 Davis Ave., Pass Christian, 228-222-4863
robinsnestinthepass.com

TIP

With so many fabulous items offered at Robin's Nest, it can be hard to decide on that perfect gift. No worries! You can purchase a gift card. Believe me, the recipient will be excited to experience the store. In fact, grab several for gift-giving—even for yourself!

SHOP PASS CHRISTIAN OLIVE OILS & VINEGAR

FOR YOUR COOKING

Any chef will tell you and any home cook: good olive oil can make all the difference in a recipe you are producing. We are blessed to have a place in Coastal Mississippi to acquire the freshest ultra-premium extra-virgin olive oils for our cooking needs.

When you enter Pass Christian Olive Oils & Vinegar, you will see containers of various olive oils that you can purchase. Make your choice and fill the bottle accordingly. Most times, an infused olive oil is my choice—from basil-infused to wild mushroom and sage-infused to Tuscan herb-infused. These are only a few of the varieties available. Gourmet olive oil is also on hand—think black or white truffle oil. Pick up some balsamic vinegar while you're there.

The staff is friendly and knowledgeable and will help answer questions or offer suggestions. When your bottle is empty, bring it back for a refill!

141 Davis Ave., Pass Christian, 228-452-9470
gulfcoastoliveoils.com

STEP INTO THE PAST FOR A UNIQUE FIND

AT ANTIQUE MAISON

Strolling through Antique Maison, you will find an eclectic mixture of antiques, collectibles, furniture, and vintage everything. It is a fantastic place to browse and lose yourself while doing so.

You can start by perusing the furniture, as it all started there: the owner's family had a business buying and selling furniture. Then move on to the myriad of other offerings. One day you might find a fabulous pair of vintage earrings or a brooch. On another day, you will find a childhood game you loved to play. Maybe a creation of handcrafted wood will catch your eye. Move on down the line, and you may stumble upon an old vinyl album you wore out because you played it so much.

There is no limit to the possibilities of what you might find, so forge ahead and unearth that special something.

111 N 2nd St., Bay St. Louis, 228-466-4848
facebook.com/antiquemaisonllc

99

SHOP 'TIL YOU DROP

AT THE MALLS OF COASTAL MISSISSIPPI

Here in Coastal Mississippi, we have several malls where you can find an abundance of shopping pleasure. Each has different anchor stores, while some of the other stores may have locations in more than one mall.

Edgewater Mall: Major stores here are Belk, Dillard's, and JCPenney. Premier Cinemas is also located here, as well as Pep Boys. Inside you will find a rock-climbing wall.

Crossroads Center: Major stores here are Barnes & Noble, Pier One Imports, Academy Sports and Outdoors, and PetSmart.

Gulfport Outlet Mall: Big-name outlets here include American Eagle Outfitters, Bath & Body Works, Banana Republic, Coach NY, and Kate Spade.

The Promenade: Here you will find Best Buy, Dick's Sporting Goods, Marshalls, and Michaels.

Edgewater Mall
2600 Beach Blvd., Biloxi, 228-388-3424
edgewatermall.com

Crossroads Center
15082 Crossroads Pkwy., Gulfport, 877-225-5337
mallsinamerica.com/mississippi/crossroads-center

Gulfport Outlet Mall
10000 Factory Shop Blvd., Gulfport, 228-867-6101
premiumoutlets.com/outlet/gulfport/stores

The Promenade
3821 Promenade Pkwy., D'Iberville, 601-261-3032
mallsinamerica.com/mississippi/the-promenade

100

FLING CAUTION TO THE WIND
AT FINDERS KEEPERS RESALE & MARKETPLACE

Start with an assortment of 75 vendors, add a touch of flea market and a spatter of a specialty store, and you come to Finders Keepers Resale & Marketplace. You truly never know what you may find here—no joke!

It is hard to describe all the items available here, and each time you visit, they will likely all be different. From a dining-room set or desk to some hard-to-find kitchen tools. Jams and jellies to vintage jewelry. Maybe even a mattress or curio cabinet. There are even home decorations and collectibles.

Each time you arrive, plan to spend hours browsing through the marketplace. On occasion, there are even outdoor vendors. So take your time and be sure to visit all the vendors. You may walk away with one item or a dozen treasures. You never know.

185 Veterans Ave., Biloxi, 228-860-1852
facebook.com/finderskeepersmarketplace

Seafood Festival

ACTIVITIES
BY SEASON

SPRING/SUMMER

FALL/WINTER

Walter Anderson mural

SUGGESTED ITINERARIES

GET BACK TO NATURE

BRING THE KIDDOS

A WEEKEND DATE

Sip a Perfect Cup of Joe at the Mockingbird Café, 14

Walk the Beach Hand in Hand to Enjoy the Coast, 57

Make Playing in the Water Better with Beach Rentals, 75

Ply the Waves on the Biloxi Schooner Sail, 63

Feel Nature's Power at the Friendship Oak and Angel Trees, 92

Browse the Shops of Century Hall, 115

Get to Know a Local Genius at the Walter Anderson Museum of Art, 82

Feast at Jourdan River Steamer, 23

Celebrate Cool Music at Ground Zero Blues Club Biloxi, 28

Dare to Win at the Beau Rivage Resort and Casino, 40

DINE WHERE THE LOCALS GO

Devour in Delight at Tato-Nut Donut Shop, 9

Chill Out with Friends at Ole Biloxi Fillin' Station, 12

Gobble Up Fabulous Crust and Toppings at Pop's Pizzeria, 2

Satisfy Your Oyster Craving at Half Shell Oyster House, 6

Pick Up Some Island Vibes at the Blind Tiger, 13

Biloxi Schooner

MISSISSIPPI
AQUARIUM

INDEX

"FRIENDSHIP OAK"
1487 -
I AM CALLED THE FRIENDSHIP OAK
THOSE WHO ENTER MY SHADOW WILL
REMAIN FRIENDS THROUGH
ALL THEIR LIFETIME.
SOPHOMORE CLASS 1969